Origins

Top Speed

John Malam

Contents

OXFORD
UNIVERSITY PRESS

A need for speed

How fast is fast?

Modern life moves at a fast pace. But not if you're a snail or a sloth.

Snails make a clear liquid called mucus to help them move. This leaves a trail behind.

The sloth is perfectly happy to be the slowest mammal on earth. It lives in trees and goes as fast as it needs to.

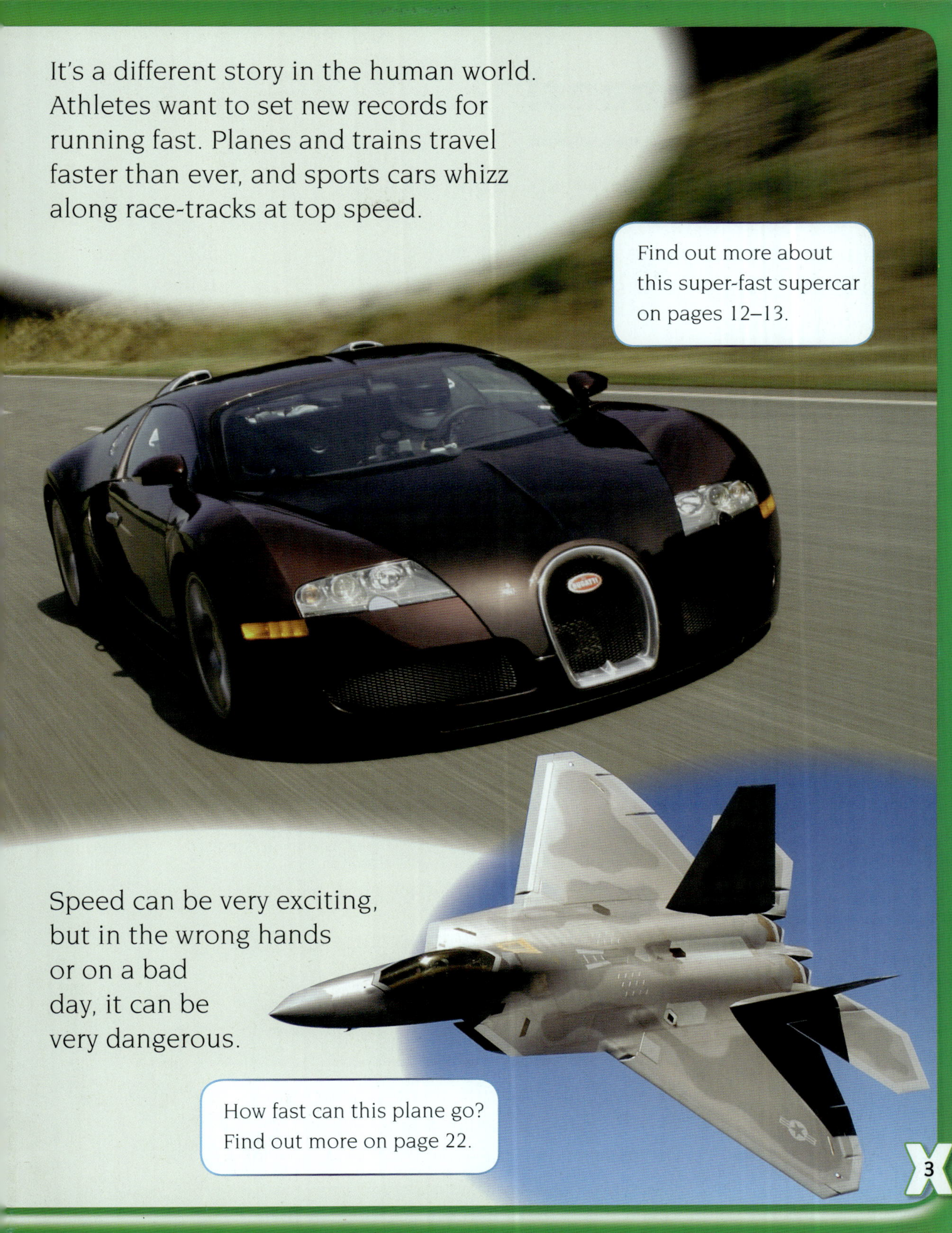

It's a different story in the human world. Athletes want to set new records for running fast. Planes and trains travel faster than ever, and sports cars whizz along race-tracks at top speed.

Find out more about this super-fast supercar on pages 12–13.

Speed can be very exciting, but in the wrong hands or on a bad day, it can be very dangerous.

How fast can this plane go? Find out more on page 22.

Super humans!

In Oxford, England, in 1954, six young men ran a race. They ran around the track four times – a distance of exactly one mile. The crowd shouted, "Go faster!" They knew something special was happening.

Roger Bannister won the race. What was his time? The timekeeper spoke. "Ladies and gentlemen," he said, "here is the result … a new world record. The time was 3 minutes 59.4 seconds."

Today's mile record-holders

	Name	Nationality	Time	Year
Men's mile	Hicham El Guerrouj	Moroccan	3 minutes 43.13 seconds	1999
Women's mile	Svetlana Masterkova	Russian	4 minutes 12.56 seconds	1996

FACT

Experts say that by the year 2026, the mile will be run in 3 minutes 30 seconds.

Roger Bannister was the first person in history to run a mile in less than 4 minutes. His achievement became known as the 'Miracle Mile'.

On your marks, get set, go!

The world's most famous human race is over in seconds. This is the 100 metres race. Super-fit, super-fast athletes **sprint** at top speed in a straight line. The difference between winning and losing can be less than a second.

100m record-holders

	Name	Nationality	Time	Year
Men's 100m	Usain Bolt	Jamaican	9.58 seconds	2009
Women's 100m	Florence Griffith Joyner	American	10.49 seconds	1988

Usain Bolt

Florence Griffith Joyner

FACT

If Usain Bolt carried on running at the same speed, he could run a mile in 2 minutes 34 seconds! (However that would be impossible because a human can't keep running that fast for that long.)

Racing with nature

Big waves and strong winds are good news for surfers, windsurfers and kitesurfers. These super-fit people love to race with nature. The waves and the wind push them across the sea.

Surfing

Some waves are as high as houses or even higher. Surfers love these big waves. As a wave swells up, the surfers stand on their surfboards. The wave pushes the surfers forwards and they skim along at top speed. It takes a lot of practice to stay on a surfboard. One surfer has ridden a wave for over 10 kilometres without falling off – that's a world record!

Windsurfing

What do you get if you put a sail onto a surfboard? A sailboard, that's what. Windsurfers use sailboards and the wind blows them across water. Windsurfing is a mixture of surfing and sailing. It can be very fast, with sailboards travelling at up to 90 kilometres per hour. Windsurfers have to balance on their boards and hold onto their sails at the same time. That's really hard to do!

Kitesurfing

If you fix a kite to a short surfboard, you turn it into a kiteboard. The kite is a power kite. It is strong enough to pull a kiteboard and the kitesurfer right out of the water! The top kitesurfers are pulled along at nearly 80 kilometres per hour.

Fantastic Formula One!

It's race day. The super-fast racing cars line up at the start of a Formula One (F1) race. The drivers want the race to start quickly, before the powerful engines in their cars overheat. They watch the red lights above the track. Suddenly, the lights go out – and that's the **signal** for the race to begin. For the next two hours the cars zoom around the race-track. They race at up to 322 kilometres per hour. How do they go so fast?

How an F1 car works

The faster you go, the faster the air around you goes. To go very fast you need the air to move out of the way very quickly.

The barge boards control the air that flows over the front wheels. The air is pushed aside to keep the car moving fast. Side pods are **vents** in the side of the car. Air flows through them to help keep the engine cool. The rear wing breaks the flow of air across the car. It stops the car going too fast!

The front wing is designed to make the air flow quickly over it.

High speed crashes look very dangerous but modern F1 cars are incredibly strong and safe.

Winners and losers

By the end of the race the cars will have driven about 300 kilometres, but not every car will finish. Some will have accidents or burst tyres or problems with their engines. Others will spin off the track and lose their place. The first eight cars to finish score points. When all the races in a year are over, the driver with the most points is the new Formula One World Champion.

FACT

F1 facts

- An F1 car is made from more than 3000 parts.
- It takes about five months to build an F1 car.
- It takes about 3.5 seconds to change all four tyres.
- An F1 car costs about £1 million to build.
- An F1 car reaches 100 kilometres per hour in about 2 seconds.

Train power

Liverpool and Manchester are two cities in England which are about 48 kilometres apart. Before 1830, people travelled between these cities in coaches pulled by horses. The journey took four and a half hours. Everything changed in 1830, when the two cities were joined by a railway line. It was the world's first railway for taking people from town to town, and it was fast!

The train that ran on the line was called *Rocket* and it raced along at up to 24 kilometres per hour. Instead of more than four hours, the journey by train took two hours.

A **replica** of the *Rocket* in a museum.

A TGV going at top speed.

Fast in France

Today, the world's fastest passenger trains are in France. They are called TGV trains. This is an **abbreviation** for the French words *train à grande vitesse* (say: tran a grahn-duh vee-tess). In English, this means 'high-speed train'. A TGV moves along the line at about 320 kilometres per hour but it can go much faster! When a TGV reached a speed of about 575 kilometres per hour, it set a record for the fastest train ever!

The car's the star!

There are cars and then there are supercars! A supercar is a sports car that can be driven on ordinary roads. Even though a supercar can go very fast, the driver mustn't go faster than the speed limit. On a race-track though, a driver may drive as fast as he or she wishes.

Supercars look great. They are very low to the ground. Most of them have smooth, sleek body shapes, which is the best shape for going fast. Just like Formula One racing cars, they have powerful engines. They are built from **carbon fibre** and titanium metal which makes them strong and light.

Only 300 of the Bugatti Veyron will be made. Each one costs £800,000 to buy!

The Gumpert Apollo. The doors of this supercar open upwards and are called 'gullwing doors'.

Top 10 Supercar speeds

Supercar	Top speed
Bugatti Veyron Super Sport	431 km/h
SSC Ultimate Aero	414 km/h
Saleen S7 Twin Turbo	399 km/h
Koenigsegg CCX	394 km/h
McLaren F1	386 km/h
Ultima GTR	372 km/h
Gumpert Apollo	360 km/h
Ferrari Enzo	355 km/h
Ascari A10	354 km/h
Jaguar XJ220	349 km/h

Designers are always working to make supercars faster so the top speed record keeps being broken!

Land speed record

Most cars today can go faster than 64 kilometres per hour. But in 1898, just a few years after the motor car was invented, people thought this was super-fast. It was the very first speed record for a car and it became known as the 'land speed record'.

The Supersonic Car

In 1997, 99 years after the first land speed record was set, a car with a jet engine zoomed into the record books. Called Thrust SSC (**SuperSonic** Car), it roared along a straight line in a desert in America. When it passed 1225 kilometres per hour a loud booming noise was heard. Thrust SSC had broken the **sound barrier**, which meant it was travelling faster than the speed of sound. This was the first time a vehicle on land had travelled at supersonic speed.

Thrust SSC was more than 16 metres long, weighed about 10 tonnes and used 18 litres of **fuel** every second!

How the land speed record has got faster		
Year	**Vehicle**	**Speed**
1965	Goldenrod	658 km/h
1965	Spirit of America	966 km/h
1970	Blue Flame	1002 km/h
1983	Thrust 2	1020 km/h
1997	Thrust SSC	1228 km/h

Blue Flame was a rocket-powered car which set a new land speed record of 1002 kilometres per hour in 1970.

Dragsters

A dragster, or drag racer, is a special type of racing car. It's made for doing one thing only – going as fast as it can in a straight line.

The fastest drag racers don't burn petrol in their engines like most other racing cars. Instead, they run on '**nitro**', which burns a lot faster than petrol. Nitro makes dragsters go at very, very fast speeds.

Drag racing can be dangerous. If the front wheels lift off the ground the car could flip over. This is called a 'blowover'.

A drag chute (like a **parachute**) slows the dragster down.

Drag racing at a glance	
How many dragsters in a race?	Two
How far do they race?	400 metres
How much fuel does a dragster use?	About 23 litres every race
How long does a race last?	4–7 seconds
Where is drag racing most popular?	In the USA

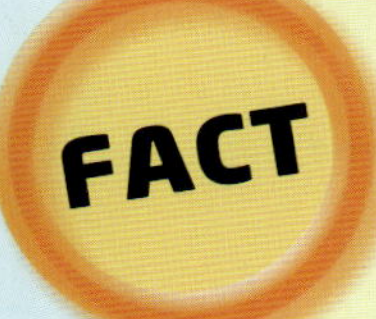

The fastest dragsters can reach speeds of more than 500 kilometres per hour!

Breaking the sound barrier

The Superfortress was a big warplane. It was a bomber, whose job was to drop bombs in wars. It had another job, too. On 14 October, 1947, instead of carrying bombs it carried a small, orange-coloured plane. The plane was called the Bell X-1. It was about to make history.

A bullet with wings

The X-1 was shaped like a bullet: round and smooth and with short wings. It was built like this to fly very fast. The Superfortress climbed high into the sky. When it got to 2100 metres above the ground, the X-1 pilot got into the cockpit. His name was Charles Yeager, but everyone called him Chuck. The X-1 was a top-secret plane that belonged to the US government. Chuck had flown it before, but this flight was going to be different from all the others.

The record-breaking Bell X-1.

Famous flight

When the Superfortress was 7000 metres high, it dropped the X-1 as planned. After that, Chuck used the X-1's rocket engine to blast it through the sky. He reached a speed of 1227 kilometres per hour – faster than the speed of sound. Chuck Yeager and the X-1 had broken through the sound barrier. The moment they did that, they were moving at supersonic speed. No one had moved this fast before.

Chuck broke the record for travelling through the air. It was another 50 years before Thrust SSC travelled this fast on land.

Name: Charles Yeager
Nickname: Chuck
Date of birth: February 13, 1923
Country: USA
Occupation: Test pilot
Famous for: First person to travel faster than the speed of sound

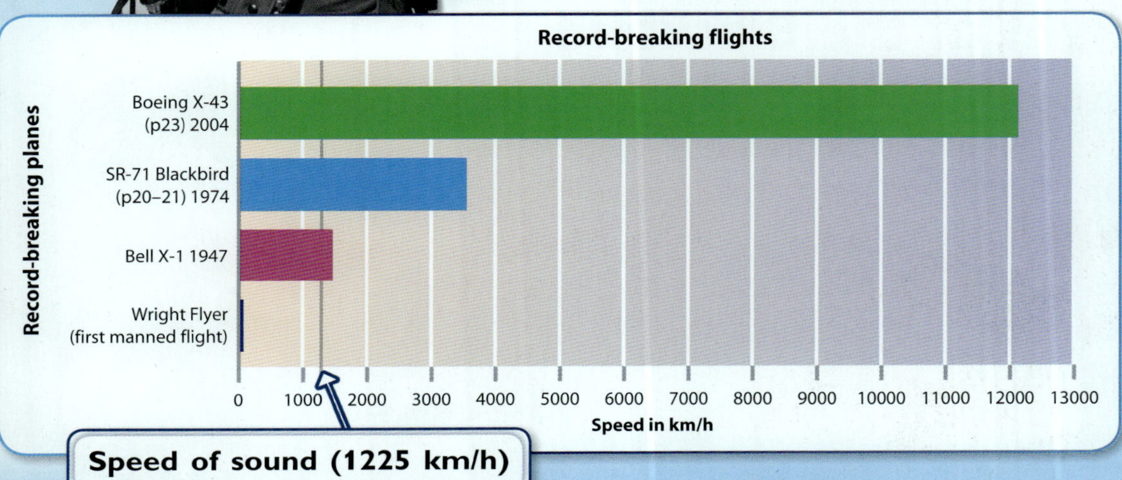

Record-breaking flight

It's about 5500 kilometres from New York, in the USA, to London, in the UK. A passenger aeroplane takes about six hours to fly between the two cities. Yet in 1974, a plane did it in less than two hours.

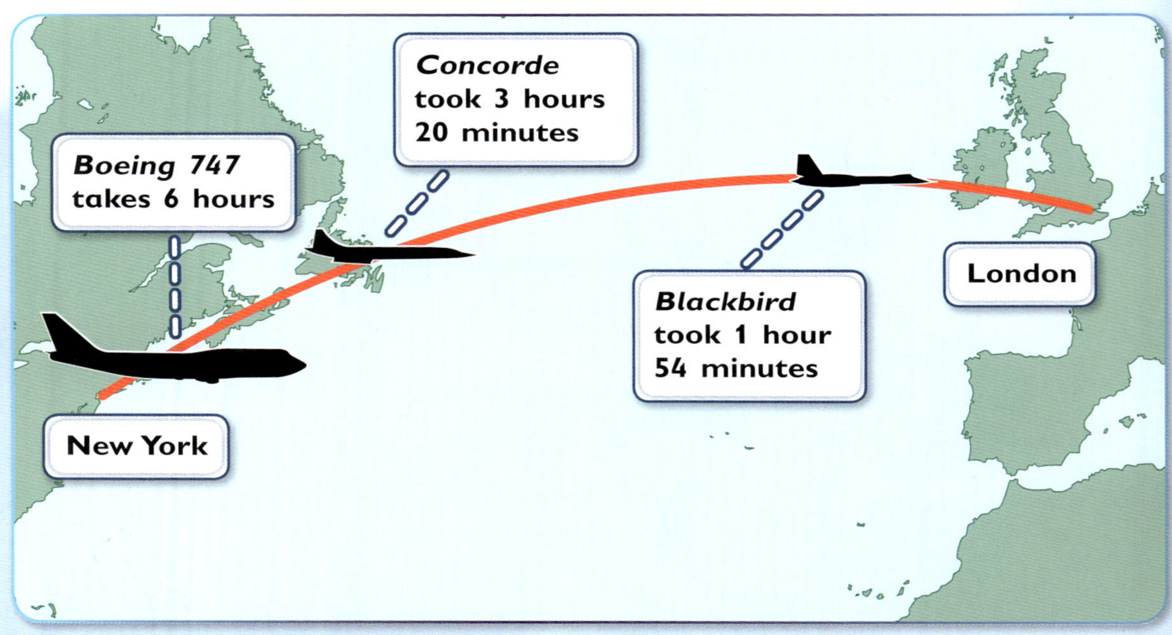

Flight of the Blackbird

The plane's name was the SR-71 but everyone called it the *Blackbird*. It was a top-secret plane that belonged to the USA. The *Blackbird* was a spy plane. Its job was to fly high and fast over other countries to find out what they were doing.

The *Blackbird* was flown to the UK, so it could take part in an air show. The plane took off from an airforce base in the USA and flew towards New York City. As it flashed over New York at 3200 kilometres per hour, the pilots started to count the time to London.

Somewhere over the Atlantic Ocean, the *Blackbird* slowed down. A big plane filled with fuel came close and the *Blackbird* refilled its tanks. Then it set off again at top speed. It took 1 hour 54 minutes 56.4 seconds to reach London. This is a record that has not been broken … yet!

FACT Blackbird pilots wore suits like the ones worn by **astronauts** in space.

The *Blackbird* in flight.

Planes of the future

The Bell X-1 plane flown by Chuck Yeager in 1947 was the first of the X-planes. The X stands for '**experimental**'.

Experimental planes

X-planes come from the USA and more than 50 different ones have been made. X-1 was the first and X-53 is the latest. They all have one thing in common – to try out something new. If the new idea works, it might be used in everyday planes.

The X-53 has wings that twist so it can move better.

The X-43 was built to test hypersonic speed.

Amazing X-planes	
Plane	**Built to test**
X-13	Taking-off straight up, like a helicopter
X-18	Wings that could be **tilted**
X-26	Flying without an engine, like a **glider**
X-40	Space plane of the future
X-43	Flying at **hypersonic** speed
X-47	Flying without a pilot at the controls

Fastest plane ever

One thing that X-planes have always tested, ever since the X-1, is flying fast. The X-1 was the very first supersonic plane but the X-43 makes it look slow. In 2004, the X-43 flew at 12 144 kilometres per hour. It is the first hypersonic plane and it can fly right around the world in less than four hours! So far, only a small version has been tested, with no one on board. Will hypersonic planes become the planes of the future?

The world's fastest boat

It's one thing to go fast on land or in the sky, but moving fast on water is an even greater challenge. The faster you go, the harder it gets, as the water slows a boat down. So what do you do? You build bigger, more powerful boats!

Ken Warby in the *Spirit of Australia*.

The Spirit of Australia

Ken Warby knows about power boats. He bought an old jet engine and fitted it to a boat he was building at his home in Australia. He called his jet-powered boat the *Spirit of Australia*. When it was ready, he raced it across a lake. Each time he raced the boat, it went faster than before. Soon, he had set a record for the fastest boat in Australia – but Ken knew his super-boat could go faster still.

Will Ken Warby's *Aussie Spirit* become the world's fastest boat?

Record-maker, record-breaker

Ken's life changed forever on 8 October, 1978. He took the *Spirit of Australia* onto the lake – and went for it! The big engine roared into action and the *Spirit of Australia* shot across the water. It reached a top speed of 511 kilometres per hour, and became the world's fastest boat.

The record has never been beaten but there's one man who thinks he can do it. It's Ken Warby, who has been testing a new boat called *Aussie Spirit*. When it's ready he wants to smash the record he set all those years ago.

The men who drove Bluebird

Malcolm Campbell

Malcolm Campbell had a dream. He wanted to be the fastest man on earth and, for a time, he was. In 1924 he drove a car called *Bluebird* along a beach in Wales. He reached 235 kilometres per hour, and set the land speed record. Over the next few years Malcolm set more records, in cars called *Bluebird*. In 1935 he set a new world land speed record of 484 kilometres per hour.

Malcolm had another wish. He wanted to be the fastest man on water and, for a time, he was. He built a powerful boat, which he called *Bluebird*. In 1939 he raced it across Coniston Water, in England. It reached 228 kilometres per hour – a world record.

Malcolm Campbell sets the land speed record in *Bluebird*.

Donald Campbell

Malcolm Campbell had a son. His name was Donald and he was also a record-breaker on land and water. His cars and boats were all called *Bluebird*. Donald Campbell is the only person in history to be top-speed king of land and water at the same time. He held both world records in 1964. Three years later he had a terrible accident. As his boat *Bluebird* flashed across Coniston Water, the boat's nose lifted up at high speed. The boat flipped over and sank. Donald was killed.

Donald Campbell's fatal crash on Coniston Water.

FACT

Bluebird lives on

In 2002, Don Wales, the grandson of Malcolm Campbell and the nephew of Donald Campbell, set a speed record for an electric car. He reached 220 kilometres per hour. The name of the car was … *Bluebird Electric 2*.

When things go wrong

Which of these words best describes 'speed':

- exciting
- fun
- dangerous
- scary?

All of these words are about speed. It's exciting to go on a fast roller coaster (and a bit scary). It's fun to run but it's dangerous to drive too fast. Sometimes things do go wrong. Here are two true stories of what happened to people who wanted to be the fastest.

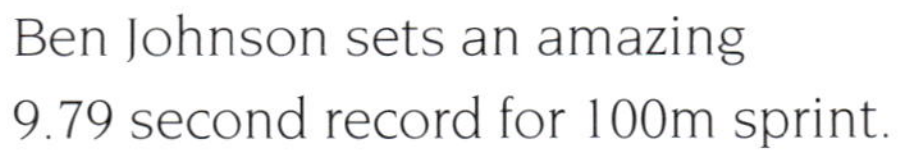

Ben Johnson sets an amazing 9.79 second record for 100m sprint.

Johnson is punished for cheating.

From winner to loser

Ben Johnson wanted to be the world's fastest runner over 100 metres. In 1988, it seemed as if he was. He won a gold medal at the Olympic Games and set a new world record of 9.79 seconds. Everyone was amazed at how fast he had run. It seemed he was a superhuman athlete.

In fact, he was a super-cheat. Johnson had taken drugs to help him run faster and he was found out. His gold medal was given to another runner and Johnson was banned from racing.

High-speed crash

On 20 September 2006, Richard Hammond crashed a car whilst travelling at 464 kilometres per hour. He was trying to set a new speed record for a car in Britain. When a front tyre on his dragster burst, the car spun out of control and crashed. Hammond was lucky to survive. Other drivers, such as Donald Campbell, who've tried to break speed records have lost their lives.

The dragster at top speed.

The dragster in pieces after its crash.

Speed: good or bad?

Is it a good thing or a bad thing to move fast?

In many ways speed is a good thing. For example:

- It's exciting to watch.
- Top athletes train hard to make their bodies fit and strong because they want to run, swim or cycle as fast as they can.
- Racing drivers want to win races and they can only do that by driving fast.
- Planes, trains and cars are going faster than ever so journey times have become shorter.

But speed can also cause problems. For example:

- Athletes can injure themselves.
- Cars, planes and trains can crash.
- Machines that travel fast need fuel, and the faster they go the more fuel they use.
- Some fuels are running out and cost a lot of money. When all the world's oil and petrol have been used up, what will we do? Perhaps someone will invent a new form of transport. Or perhaps we'll have to learn to live more slowly.

Former world-record holder, Asafa Powell was injured in this race.

Glossary

abbreviation	a short way of writing or saying a word
astronaut	someone who travels in space
carbon fibre	a very strong and light material
experimental	testing an idea to see whether it works
fuel	anything that people burn to give heat or power
glider	a type of aeroplane without an engine
hypersonic	a very fast speed, about five times faster than the speed of sound
nitro	short for 'nitromethane', it is a fuel used in drag racing
parachute	a large piece of material that opens to slow down a person or vehicle
replica	an exact copy
signal	a light, sound or movement that tells people what they should do, or tells them that something is going to happen
sound barrier	the point at which a vehicle's speed is the same as the speed of sound
sprint	to run as fast as you can over a short distance
supersonic	faster than the speed of sound
tilt	to tip something up so that it slopes
vents	slits in the side of a car

Index